SAM ARNOLD's
FRYINGPANS WEST

Illustrated by Carrie Forman Arnold

To Chuck & Barbara
May your trails be free of
grizzlies and your pot full of
Buffalo!

Carrie Arnold   *The Fort*
Sept. 22
1987

Published by
Arnold and Company
2221 South Fillmore
Denver, Colorado 80210

Design and production by Håkan Carheden
Cover painting "Range Breakfast, 1885" by C. F. Arnold
Photograph of cover art by Lloyd Rule
Type set in Lubalin Graph by Typography Plus/Denver
Printing by Mutual Graphics, Denver
Paper: 80 lbs Lustro Offset Enamel Dull Cream Cover,
80 lbs Gainsborough Wheat Text
supplied by Zellerbach Paper Company

11th Edition

ISBN 0-914454-03-X
Printed in the United States of America

INTRODUCTION TO THE NEW REVISED EDITION

Already over 100,000 copies of **Fryingpans West** in English have sold in the U.S. and Canada. So, we felt it was time to bring to you an updated, enlarged, and illustrated version which will show the results now of more than two decades of research into the foods and drinks of the West. To the many fine historians, including my wife Carrie, who have helped with this book, I lift my cup in the Mountain Man's Toast . . .

> Here's to the childs what's come afore,
> An here's to the pilgrims what comes after,
> May yer trails be free of Grizzlies,
> Yer packs filled with plews,
> And fat buffler in yer pot!

Sam Arnold

PREFACE

The most frequent question asked of me is how I became interested in food and drink of the early West. Though I've always had an adventuresome palate and enjoyed amateur cooking, the serious beginning point came in 1962. I'd bought some land in the foothills southwest of Denver. By sheerest chance, I came across a picture of Bent's Old Fort, an historic fur trade fort of early Colorado. It looked like a castle, made of adobe bricks. The idea of living in a fort fascinated me, and shortly I began construction of a full-sized replica to serve as my home. Within a year it was completed, but, in order to pay the large mortgage, it was decided to turn a large part of the building into a restaurant.

Jumping into the restaurant business was an education. I really had to learn to cook. This meant cooking for several hundred persons at a time. My research into the history of Bent's Fort and the fur trade brought me to reading over 2,000 journals and diaries of the period. Sure enough, one of the most written-about facets of life in those days was mealtime. Possibly the most outlandish recipe was "mouffle." This is boiled moose nose. I had asked my game purveyor in Montana to save me some moose noses, for I had read about a favorite dish of the French-Canadian trapper called "mouffle," and I was determined to try it. The noses arrived, each about three feet long and covered with thick hair. According to the recipe I'd found in Canada, the cook was instructed to put the nose on a stick and hold it over the fire until the hair burned off. I built a fire on the courtyard of The Fort, and that evening customers walking by saw me roasting a long, ugly, hairy nose over the fire. The smell was hideous. Later I brushed it clean with a wire brush and soaked it overnight in salt water to remove any burnt hair flavor.

The moose nose was then boiled with a bit of onion, bay leaf, peppercorn and salt. It turned out to be dull in flavor, extremely bland, and somewhat like a pickled pig's foot in consistency. I put it on the menu for $1.50 per portion, served cold, sliced, and with a piquant sauce. One evening a disbelieving guest wagered $100.00 to another that the "boiled moose nose" on the menu wasn't *really* moose nose. He lost.

Remember too, that cooking isn't a science. It's an art that comes from a familiarity with the characteristics of your ingredients combined with your own creative touch. Recipes are only like roadmaps—how you travel and where you end up depends on you. Good luck . . .

Sam Arnold

4

ABOUT THE AUTHOR

In 1968, KRMA-TV, Denver's educational TV station approached Sam Arnold to write and host a series of ½-hour shows in color on early western food and drink. Mr. Arnold's reputation in 19th-century cookery was then already widespread. Mr. Arnold had made practical application of many of the recipes in his western restaurant, THE FORT, located southwest of Denver near Morrison, Colorado.

Sam Arnold has been a speaker at the national conferences of the Western History Association; The National Wildlife Federation; and for the Smithsonian Institution; he has been cited by the American Association for State and Local History; and has authored many articles and books on western history. In addition to his interest in western history, Sam Arnold has other talents. He is an accomplished photographer, and musician. Folk and classical music are favorites, and he plays well on both mandolin and musical saw.

Mr. Arnold is a noted chef having been featured in *Bon Appetit* magazine's ``Great Kitchens, Great Cooks'' series and the Ouray, Colorado, Culinary Arts Show for many years. He has travelled extensively, photographing and writing about foods of different regions for magazines and television. His travels have included the Soviet Union, most of western Europe, Central and South America, Southeast Asia, Japan and mainland China. He is an accomplished instructor in many of the world's cuisines and has taught western American cooking in Germany. He and his wife Carrie, an accomplished artist, have also attended cooking schools in Paris, Sri Lanka, Thailand, and Taiwan.

He has also, for some years, served the Adolph Coors Brewing Company as a public relations consultant in the food field.

The FRYINGPANS WEST series of cooking shows has now been viewed in virtually every state of the U.S. It is distributed by PBS Library in Washington, D.C., to public television stations across the nation, adding a new dimension to America's understanding of its historic past.

CONTENTS

Meats coming West

Salt Pork . . . basic staple pioneer food.

In the meat department of virtually every supermarket in the country, one finds little packets of salt pork, all neatly wrapped and priced. They don't move rapidly and are bought only by the occasional cook who uses salt pork for flavoring for beans or soup. Yet, in the westward migration, salt pork was the mainstay of the trappers, explorers, and wagon train migrants.

Why was salt pork such a basic food? Because, it was preserved with the salt and could travel without spoilage; it could be used to flavor other bland food; and because it was easy to fix.

Back in the days of the Oregon migration in the late 1840's, some enterprising authors without personal experience of having traveled the trail themselves, wrote immigrant booklets telling the prospective pioneer what he should take with him in order to survive the long arduous trip. These booklets were bought by thousands of persons wanting information, but they were often terribly misleading. They stated that one should take several hundred pounds of salt pork per person. By the time wagons, loaded with provisions, rolled up to Fort Laramie in eastern Wyoming, the horses were exhausted from pulling such weight. The settlers dumped their excess provisions, and many tons of salt pork were left behind at Fort Laramie.

Even further back in time, the famed Lewis and Clark expedition, exploring the Louisiana Territory to the West Coast, carried salt pork as a staple. The French-Canadian *voyageurs*, paddling through the north country rivers and lakes, also kept salt pork which they cooked with dried split peas. They made a fire early in the morning, and stoked the coals into a pile. A few slabs of sliced salt pork, a mess of split peas and water went into a big iron pot. This would be buried in the coals and left until the end of the day. Slowly simmered all day long, the dish was a famous *voyageur* mainstay — and a good easy one for anyone today.

VOYAGEURS' PEA SOUP

2 cups dried yellow split peas
cold water
6 oz. salt pork

1 medium onion studded with 2 whole cloves
2 medium red potatoes, diced
Black pepper and salt to taste

Soak peas overnight after having picked over them for rocks or other inedible debris. Put into Dutch oven in the morning with enough water to cover. Add the onion, potatoes and salt pork. Dig a hole deeper than the Dutch oven height, and fill partly with hot coals. Lower Dutch oven into hole and cover top with more coals ("between two fires"). Mound dirt around oven and partially over lid and coals. Let it cook throughout the day and by evening you will find a hearty meal. If cooked on a stove, the heat should be more concentrated and time required will be 2½ to 3 hours of simmering.

FRIED SALT PORK.

½ lb. per person salt pork
   (cut into ½" thick strips)
2 tablespoons flour

salt
pepper
1 cup milk

Cut the salt pork strips into bite-sized pieces. Pour two kettles of boiling water over the salt pork to remove much of the salty taste. Discard this briny water. If you think of it, soak the salt pork the night before, changing water once or twice; however, the boiling water works pretty well. Pat dry. Fry the salt pork pieces, then reserve. With some of the fat in the pan, add the flour, mix, and brown. Next add milk and stir to make a cream gravy. Salt and pepper to taste. Add back the fried salt pork. Serve this with HOPPING JOHN. It makes a good easy Sunday supper, a fast lunch, or a good side dish for breakfast.

HOPPING JOHN was always served in the South on New Year's Day by tradition in order to bring good luck for the coming 12 months. The story is told that children would hop around the dining table at New Year's Day dinner and would be served HOPPING JOHN.

Susan Magoffin, 1846 Santa Fe Trail traveler

HOPPING JOHN

½ lb. slab bacon

2 qts. water

2 cups black-eyed peas

1 cup rice, long-grain or minute

½ cup coconut, shredded

Cook the bacon in water for about one half hour, then add black-eyed peas and rice. Simmer until peas are soft. Then add coconut, and simmer at lowest heat for another 15 minutes. Lift out the bacon and slice. Drain the peas and rice, and pop into the oven for a few minutes to dry until rice is fluffy. Serve with the bacon sliced on top.

Try frying the bacon until nearly crisp, to get a toasty bacon flavor. Then cut pieces into 1" lengths and serve over top. It's a good variation found often in the ranch houses of the early west.

I also like FRIED SALT PORK served over HOPPING JOHN. Just leave out the bacon, although the bacon does give a fine flavor to the rice.

Another favorite dish of the old west was BROILED MARROW BONES.

Trappers sitting around the fire took hip and leg bones of the buffalo, split them open and roasted the marrow. Sopped up with some good sourdough bread, hot from the oven, this was called "prairie butter". Both Indians and trappers alike considered marrow an important food. It was eaten cooked, spread over bread, and used in soups and stews. Even a type of dessert was made with berries and marrow cooked together. Marrow-eating was popular in England too

10

and some gourmet restaurants there still serve broiled marrow bones as a savoury. In antique stores you can find special marrow scoops . . . a spoon with a long gouge-shape to it.

BROILED MARROW BONES

For your next party, ask your butcher to run some large beef thigh bones through his electric saw lengthwise to lay open the marrow. Pop these, marrow side up, into a 450° oven for a few minutes until the marrow is barely brown. Then serve these huge thigh bones to your guests with fresh hot bread. Let them spread it on the bread as you would butter. It's delicious!

Hikers and mountain climbers have recently discovered an early American food that provides energy and good eating . . . JERKY.

Sun drying of meat isn't new anywhere on the globe, but only in recent years has good jerky come onto the market in quantity. Jerky is light in weight . . . consequently good for the camper or hiker to carry. It's easy to make, but most people don't know how to cut a block of meat into strips.

In butchering, the Indian followed the natural contours and muscle layers. He did not cut cross grain, or saw through bones the way modern butchers do. Indians and the early mountain men often refused to eat cross grain cut meat.

JERKY

To cut jerky, a very thin, flat, razor-sharp knife is needed. A hunting knife is too thick. A knife sharpened on one side only is the best to use. Cut the large chunk of meat into a rectangle or square (approximately 3 or 4" square.) Next, cut the cube almost in half to within ¼" of bottom of meat, cross grain. Hold chunk of meat firmly to table and turn knife in the cut to a flat position slowly cutting away at the bottom . . . no more than ¼" thick with the grain, as if you were unrolling a jelly roll; maintaining a ¼" thickness. (In a way, it's like peeling an orange from the inside.)

11

One chunk of meat will turn into a strip, sometimes three or four feet long. Take skewers (plum or cherry wood is good, or the bamboo ones used for outdoor barbecuing). Hang these strips, skewered on each end, high on poles so the dogs won't get them. I usually put a piece of cheesecloth over the top to keep the flies away . . . but they rarely settle on the meat anyway, since it is cut so thin. In hot sun, it will dry in a couple of days. Take inside at night so that it won't absorb moisture from the atmosphere and put in a clean cloth or towel. In cloudy or rainy weather you can hang it indoors where there is good air circulation. The Indians never added salt or pepper to the meat. You can, if you want to, and peppered jerky is good eating. My favorite is to dredge the meat in an equal mix of Jamaican Pickapeppa sauce, and Lingham's Chilly Sauce. I put it in an open oven on the racks, and set a fan in front of the stove to run all night. No heat, but lots of air. By morning it'll be jerked.

Not only can you eat jerky in its natural state, but when camping, you can break it up, boil it in water and eat the meat stew. It absorbs the liquid and becomes plump and tasty. Salt the stew to taste, add prairie turnips, or potatoes and regular white onions. You can buy commercially made jerky in many taverns, but often it is simply a meat mash that has been extruded into strips, then baked. It is not real jerky and does not taste as good as the real thing. WASHTUNKALA was a Sioux Indian stew. While filming the "Fryingpans West" TV show at Rosebud Indian Reservation, I discovered WASHTUNKALA. It is a delicious corn stew made with dried deer or buffalo meat. Corn dried the year before "on the cob" was shucked and placed into a large glass jar with water overnight. The jars were only filled about two-thirds with the corn for when it absorbed the water it would swell, filling the jar. Strangely, it tasted almost as good as fresh corn again. The re-hydrated corn was then thrown into a big kettle over the fire with water and bite-size pieces of dried meat, wild onions and prairie potatoes were added. The prairie potatoes taste somewhat like turnips and are often strung like garlics by the old Sioux people.

WASHTUNKALA

2 lbs. JERKY (beef, deer or buffalo)
   broken into bite-size pieces
2 onions, cut up (even better,
   8 small wild onions)
4 cups kernel corn, if dried,
   reconstituted with water

2 doz. prairie potatoes soaked
   overnight if dried
or 2 doz. little new potatoes
   soaked overnight if dried

Dried Prairie Potatoes

Cook together and add no salt or pepper if you want the true Indian taste.

A fun item to make for camping out is real INDIAN PEMMICAN. The true Indian way is to use chokecherries . . . a blue-black, ball-shaped, wild cherry with a large pit and little meat. It grows by waterways and the cherries come in clusters. It has a puckery flavor to the mouth but when perfectly ripe, is sweet and delicious. Indians gather these chokecherries and dry them, making a mash of cherry and cracked stones which is allowed to dry in the sun in little patties. Before use these are broken up still further with a wooden mallet, then added to water for making WASNAH (more on that later). When making PEMMICAN, use the fresh berry. Sweet cherries are a close substitute for chokecherries. In the Indian way, the chokecherry pits were rarely removed, being more often ground fine. This added a certain gritty texture to the PEMMICAN which some like . . . I don't!

INDIAN PEMMICAN

1 lb. white suet (best from around kidneys)
2 cups cherries (fresh or frozen) pitted

24 sticks JERKY or about 1 lb.
   dried meat

13

Roast sticks of jerky in the oven until they're crisp like bacon. Pound, or put through a meat grinder, along with an equal amount of the fine white fat from around calf kidneys. Also put cherries through the grinder with a little sugar. Mix together cherries, jerky and fat. Form into balls the size of chicken eggs. You can melt a little of the beef suet over the fire in a pan, and pour or pat over the pemmican balls. Placed in plastic bags, they will be longlasting. They're good eating, extremely nourishing, and make a good snack for the kids, too. This was the "iron ration" of the Sioux Indian warriors.

Herds of buffalo once covered the nation from coast to coast. With the advent of the "white eyes," hunting with heavy guns, mass destruction of the mighty bison became commonplace. By the 1840's, buffalo could only be found west of the Mississippi. By the 1860's, only the large herds of the remote northern plains states remained. By 1883, buffalos were virtually extinct. Buffalo-killing train excursions brought hunters West, and the animals were shot from the windows of the passenger cars.

It was said that, at the end of the 19th century, one could walk alongside the Northern Pacific Railroad tracks in North Dakota and never put one's foot on the ground for a distance of one hundred miles . . . walking on a carpet of dry buffalo bones.

Freight car loads of buffalo tongues, salted or smoked for preservation, went East and to Europe. The buffalo tongue and the hide were the only items generally prized by the white hunters. BUFFALO TONGUE was perhaps the greatest delicacy of the 19th Century. A favorite of both President Ulysses S. Grant and Swedish singer Jenny Lind, bison tongue was served at all the finest restaurants including famed Delmonico's in New York. Bison tongues were exported to Europe. BUFFALO TONGUE is delicious. Smoother in texture than beef tongue, it makes a splendid dish when boiled.

BUFFALO TONGUE, FORT STYLE

buffalo tongue

1 teaspoon peppercorns

dash of salt

½ cup onion, grated

2 bay leaves (laurel)

Slow-boil meat with the peppercorns, salt, onion, and bay leaves for two hours. Then, slice it thin, either hot or cold, and serve with this sauce:

CAPER SAUCE FOR BUFFALO TONGUE

1 cup mayonnaise

2 tablespoons capers

1 tablespoon horseradish (hot)

pinch of oregano and black pepper

Combine mayonnaise, capers, horseradish, oregano, and a dash of black pepper. Serve this cold sauce over the sliced tongue. (This sauce is equally good with beef tongue.)

By 1910 there were only 256 buffalo known alive on the earth, and interestingly enough, one of these was in a zoo in Calcutta, India. Through massive conservation efforts, the buffalo were saved. Today public and private herds total more than 60,000 animals.

Buffalo meat is somewhat sweeter and richer tasting than beef. Because the buffalo is not bred for meat production as is beef, fewer prime cuts are available, and the price of buffalo steak is much higher. Buffalo has less cholesterol content than beef. The mountain men boasted that one could "eat two to three times as much buffalo as beef without being a glutton on that account." One man commented that "buffalo tastes like beef wished it tasted!"

From about 1880 when the buffalo herds were cut down until about 1960, only a few bison were available for consumption. For years, the only buffalo sold were a few old animals being culled out of publicly owned herds. These would be turned over to service clubs for "Buffalo Barbecues". Almost inevitably this resulted in a bad name for buffalo meat. Stringy, tough, and strong, the old meat rarely made friends, especially when over-cooked out of doors. When I began serving prime buffalo T-bones from two-year-old animals at my restaurant, it was a miracle. When you once put a tooth to a tender buffalo T-bone or filet, you find a whole new world.

A few years ago I was rummaging through my family's attic looking for old books. One turned up, called *THE AMERICAN COOKBOOK*, dated 1885. Among many interesting recipes was BEEFSTEAK AND OYSTERS and it was credited as a specialty of the famed Palace Hotel in early-day San Francisco. The Palace was the "Waldorf of the Pacific," and played host to many greats including the last King of Hawaii and President Grant. Here is the recipe with amounts per portion.

BEEFSTEAK AND OYSTERS

½ cup oysters (fresh)
a steak of your choice
2 tablespoons butter
1½ tablespoons flour
water or beef stock

½ fresh lime, juiced
salt and pepper
garlic salt
red pimento, chopped
parsley, chopped

In a saucepan, cook fresh oysters in butter until their edges curl. Add flour to the sauce, stirring in carefully to prevent lumps. After this roux cooks for several minutes, add a little meat stock or water to thin to a medium thick gravy. Juice the lime, add; then salt and pepper to taste. Season with a little garlic salt. In the meantime, broil a steak of your choice. Pour the oyster sauce over the steak, and garnish with colorful, chopped pimento and parsley.

This is a superb combination which may well have been invented by a Chinese cook at the Palace. The Chinese like to use the beef-oyster mix of flavors. The small, bay oysters of the West Coast are excellent in flavor and should be used where possible.

Perhaps the greatest fort in all the west was Fort Laramie in eastern Wyoming, close to the Nebraska border. It was THE important stopping point on the Oregon Trail and during the mass movement west in 1849 as many as 6,000 persons a day stopped at the fort enroute to California and the Northwest. Famed western painter, Alfred Jacob Miller, sketched the original fur trade fort which was later replaced by a government military complex. Today, it is one of the most interesting of our National Park Service sites. A number of the buildings have been restored and furnished as they originally were. The Bachelor Officers' Quarters was called ``Old Bedlam.'' In the years of this century after the fort was abandoned by the military, Old Bedlam deteriorated until it was simply waiting for a high wind to blow it over.

In 1963, a total restoration was completed by the National Park Service. As a special privilege, one night my wife and I were allowed to throw our sleeping bags down in an unfinished upstairs rear room. The house creaked and there were strange sounds which frightened my wife. I poo-poo'd them and soon she was asleep. As I lay there awake, I began to hear the distant sound of a band playing dance music as if heard across a lake from a distant band stand. It continued for some time then faded away. This was more than curious for Fort Laramie is in a remote area with no bands playing . . . and certainly not out there at three in the morning!

Elizabeth Burt was the wife of a colonel who was second in command of Fort Laramie. She wrote a cookbook which is now in the possession of the library at the fort. They very generously made available the famous FORT LARAMIE CHICKEN SALAD from her cookbook for our TV show. And here's the recipe with Elizabeth's own instructions. It tends to be a drier and more interesting chicken salad than the ones found in today's deli's.

FORT LARAMIE CHICKEN SALAD

1 tsp, dry, ground mustard
1 egg
1 ⅓ tablespoons wine or cider vinegar
6 tablespoons salad oil
1 tablespoon lemon juice
1 chicken, boiled
3 eggs, hard-boiled

3 cups celery, chopped (or young cabbage with 1 tsp. extract of celery)
1 saltspoon salt (½ tsp.)
lettuce
parsley
2 tablespoons capers, drained
1 cup olives, pitted black or green, drained

"Mix 1 heaping teaspoon fine mustard, the yolk of a fresh egg and a teaspoon of fresh wine or cider vinegar into a smooth paste using a silver fork. Measure out 6 tablespoons pure salad oil and 1 tablespoon each of vinegar and lemon juice. Mix slowly, making a creamy paste. (Adding the oil last, stirring in a few drops at a time.) Take a cold boiled chicken, remove the skin, bones and fat, and chop . . . not too fine. Cut up an equal bulk of celery, mix with the chicken. Add a saltspoon (about ½ teaspoon) salt and half of the dressing. Cover the bottom of the platter with the larger leaves of lettuce, and lay the smaller green leaves around the border. Place the salad in the dish and pour the remainder of the dressing over it. Garnish with parsley, capers, olives and hard-boiled eggs. If celery cannot be found, use white tender cabbage mixed with a teaspoon of extract of celery."

At my fort, we evolved a variation on a Mexican "SWISS ENCHILADA". In Mexico many dishes are termed "Swiss" because they have dairy products in them. The typical Mexican swiss enchiladas simply are rolled corn tortillas filled with chicken meat and onions, topped with red chile sauce, capped with sour cream. These are tasty and may be varied by mixing chopped green chiles into heated sour cream and grated Monterey Jack cheese. A dash of salt and Worcestershire sauce will turn it into a splendid sauce and if you want to make them traditionally "New Mexico style", place your corn tortillas flat and sandwich layers of chicken meat and chopped onions between them, three tortillas high. Flood the top with the sour cream, cheese, green chile sauce and place momentarily under a hot broiler to brown the top. If you can obtain them, use blue Indian cornmeal tortillas. These are available in New Mexico and some gourmet stores, frozen. They have a more primitive corn taste.

When we had large banquets of 50 to 700 persons at The Fort, it was necessary to have big casseroles . . . each to serve 40 or 50 persons. This is how The Fort SWISS ENCHILADA was created. All of the ingredients have been used together for many centuries in Mexico, but you will find it is a spectacularly good dish. BON APPETIT Magazine, America's leading gourmet monthly, photographed this dish in my kitchen in stages of preparation for an article. You may make variations to your pleasure.

SWISS ENCHILADA

24 corn tortillas
1 cooked chicken, or 2 lbs.
  raw lobster or shrimp
3 onions, thinly sliced
10 green chile strips
  (fresh peeled poblanos or
  mild canned green chiles)
1 lb. Monterey Jack cheese

2 lb. longhorn cheese
1 pint sour cream
1 quart milk or cream
garlic salt
1 tablespon oregano
1 cup pitted ripe olives
½ lb. butter
strips of red pimento

Line a large (10-12 quart) buttered, casserole with corn tortillas. Overlap them to cover the casserole bottom and sides completely. Scatter small pieces of meat from one cooked chicken over the tortillas. (Lobster or shrimp are also good meats to use and make a fine dish.) In another pot, heat sour cream, garlic salt, oregano, milk and butter until warm. Next scatter a layer of thin-sliced onion over all. Then add green chile strips cut into small pieces and cover with a half-inch layer of the grated cheeses. Add half of sour cream/milk mix, spread over all. Cover with another layer of corn tortillas . . . and if your casserole is large enough, repeat the whole process with a second layer of everything. Bake in a hot 425° oven for about 1 hour, until well-heated throughout. Before serving, place a layer of cheese over the top. Use an overhead broiler, if available, to let it melt and brown well. Garnish with pimento strips and black olive. The consistency should be damp with the melted cheese and tortillas, but not sloppy. Serves 15-20 persons.

Freshwater fish and seafood

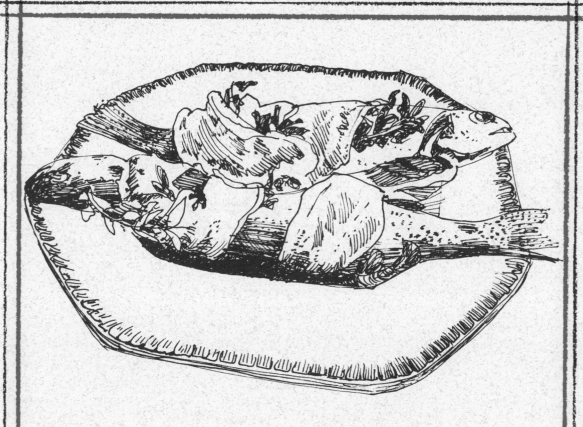

Taos Minted Trout

Fish was enjoyed by the mountain man and explorer coming West. Buffalo and deer meat (only called venison by Eastern "greenhorns") became tiresome, and a good fish dinner was a pleasant change.

The western streams and lakes provided trout, whitefish, catfish, sturgeon and other varieties which were either pan-fried or broiled on sticks over the campfires. Smoke-cooking was common, too. This is done by building a covered box of branches and leaves over a smouldering fire. Aspen wood, hickory, or apple makes a fine smoke flavor. The fish is impaled from the tail through the body to the mouth with a green branch, keeping the fish away from direct fire. After a day's smoking, nothing is better eating!

A New Mexican Indian recipe was given me by Mrs. Mary Schlosser, a Taos Indian, for MINTED TROUT. Amounts are given, per serving.

MINTED TROUT

1 trout, fresh
mint, wild or garden variety

½ cup olive or cooking oil
2 strips of bacon

Mix either garden or fresh wild mint (yerba buena) with salt and olive or cooking oil. Mash the mint with a spoon to release the flavor in the oil. Then fill the cavity of a trout with the oily mint leaves. Also wrap the trout with mint leaves and bind with one or two strips of bacon (according to the size of the trout). Secure the bacon with a round toothpick. Broil over charcoal, or under a broiler until the bacon is cooked. The bacon will baste the trout with its oils and flavor, and the mint will release its herbal taste to the trout, too. To serve, remove the mint from the trout. It will not taste sweet, but will have a strange mystical herb taste that's mighty fine eating.

Oysters were frequently eaten in the American West. They were brought west by wagon freight, and were kept cold with ice from the local ice house at each stop. Salt water and corn meal were poured down through the barrels of oysters to feed them. They stayed fat and healthy. A six to eight-inch oyster was commonplace in the 19th Century. Susan Magoffin described eating cold oysters and drinking champagne in Santa Fe on August 31, 1846. Lincoln was famous in Illinois for his oyster roasts given to the voters at election time.

A special favorite of many nineteenth-century American presidents was a PICKLED OYSTER dish. President U.S. Grant liked them better than almost any other food.

PICKLED OYSTERS

100 large oysters (ask for "counts"
   as opposed to the smaller
   "standards"
1 tablespoon salt
1 pint cider vinegar

2 sticks cinnamon
1 teaspoon allspice
½ teaspoon cloves
1 teaspoon peppercorns
1 hot red pepper, fresh or dried

Put the large oysters and their liquor into a pot, with enough water to just cover, and cook until they barely begin to boil. Add a little salt. Skim off the scum on top; then remove the oysters, and set them aside to cool. Add vinegar to the juice, the pepper without seeds, and the other spices. Heat this to a boil to release the flavor of the spices. Put the oysters in jars and pour the hot pickling juice over them. Cool and keep in the refrigerator. They will be ready to eat within two days and are delicious!

Almost every hotel, inn and restaurant in the nineteenth-century West had a wide range of condiments, catsups, and sauces available for the diner. Frequently these helped to make food palatable. One historic catsup that has passed from the scene is OYSTER CATSUP. It is easy to make and delicious with many meat dishes.

OYSTER CATSUP

1 pint oysters with liquor
1 cup sherry wine
1 tablespoon salt

1 teaspoon cayenne pepper
1 teaspoon mace

Scald 1 pint oysters in their liquor with 1 cup sherry wine. Strain the oysters and chop them fine and add salt, cayenne pepper and mace. Add this again to the liquid in which the oysters had been cooked, and boil for five minutes. Skim well, and run the whole through a sieve. When cold, bottle and seal.

A famous California oyster recipe is called HANGTOWN FRY. According to legend, a miner in 1849 from gold diggin's called Shirttail Bend, found his way into the town of Hangtown (today, Placerville). The Cary House Hotel was the only eating emporium in the area, and the miner demanded the most expensive meal they had. Eggs and oysters being the highest items in price (eggs cost over one dollar each, and oysters were astronomical in price), the cook whipped up this dish.

HANGTOWN FRY

1 dozen oysters
salt and pepper
½ cup flour, seasoned with
   black pepper

9 eggs
some red and green pepper pieces
   for garnish
¼ lb. butter

Dry the oysters on a paper towel. Dip each in salt and pepper-seasoned flour, then in one beaten egg. Finally dip into a bowl of cracker crumbs. Fry in butter until crumbs are browned. Beat 8 eggs and pour into the fryingpan in which the oysters remain. Cook slowly until firm. Serve open-face. A garnish of red and green chopped pepper pieces, sprinkled in while eggs are soft, adds color and taste.

It's basically a fried oyster omelet, but with the small Pacific Coast Olympia oysters, a little salt and freshly-ground pepper, a feast for a king!

We've had more fun with ROCKY MOUNTAIN OYSTERS than any other single food. One eastern guest at The Fort badgered a waitress, to know where Rocky Mountain Oysters came from. She finally blurted out, "They're bulls' balls!" And it was the truth . . . Rocky Mountain Oysters in Colorado are calf testicles taken at castrating time. In sheep circles, you'll find sheep "fries", also very popular, and served as "mountain oysters" frequently in Texas. The testicles of tom turkey are also highly prized and in my estimation, the most tasty of them all. They are known in the trade as "turkey surprises", perhaps because of the turkey's mystified look after the operation! (Actually, they're taken when the turkey is processed.)

At castration time on the range, the "fries" are sometimes simply impaled on a stick and toasted over the fire till cooked. This is reputed to be the best way of eating "mountain oysters".

ROCKY MOUNTAIN OYSTERS

4 lbs. Rocky Mountain Oysters (ask for veal fries, lamb or turkey) frozen
1 egg, beaten
2 cups soda cracker crumbs
2 cups cooking oil

Dip the frozen balls into warm water. This loosens the tough outer skin which must be removed from the gland. If there is other flesh still attached, cut it away. Ring the ball with a sharp knife cutting through the skin only, as you might ring an orange in order to peel it. Work your fingers under the cut and pull off the outer skin. It requires a little working loose of the gland from the outer skin. Then, before it thaws further, slice it off in ½" thick slices. Dredge in flour, then beaten egg, then in cracker crumbs. Fry in cooking oil. Fry only until crumbs are browned as overcooking will make them tough. You may also simply dredge them in seasoned flour and fry in oil.

If you prefer to charbroil them, dip them in oil and lay them across a screen over the fire, so that they will not drop through. Turn them once and do not over-cook. Serve with toothpicks and a piquant chile sauce for dipping. Sprinkle them with my special seasoning salt:

WESTERN SEASONING SALT

¼ cup garlic salt

¼ cup ground black pepper

¼ cup lemon crystals (citric acid crystals or sour salt, ground fine)

Mix ingredients and store in a convenient shaker.

26

All-powerful Chile

Kit Carson's House in Taos, New Mexico

The first Americans coming to New Mexico were greeted with a shocking new culinary experience, the chile pepper. Although black pepper and red cayenne pepper were well-known in European cultures, the red chile as found in the Southwest was a totally new experience. Then as now, Americans usually found the initial meeting was a hot and unpleasant one. After repeated exposure to the chile pod, however, most people become virtual addicts. I am one of these chile addicts. I find most meals without chile in some form as bland as a meal without salt. After eating a bowl of good hot red or green chile, one has an unusual sense of contentment and tranquility.

Chiles grow in many variations of size and type—from the tiny chile piquin and the miniature raisin chiles to the larger two or three-inch long, green jalapenos; and finally, in size to the big chile poblano, which is a seven or eight-inch long green or red pepper pod. The only difference between the red and green chile pod is that when allowed to fully ripen, the green pod turns red. There is, however, a different flavor to each. Pods may be used fresh, dried, canned, or frozen.

Taking the shiny hard outer skin off may be done by toasting the pod over a fire, or under a broiler until the skin blisters. I roast chiles under the electric broiler turning them frequently until the skin is puffed and browned. Be sure to cut off the end of the chile or pierce it so that the steam can escape. Otherwise you will find chile pieces blown over your oven. Next, while still hot, drop the pods into a sealable plastic bag, then place it in the deep freeze for 15 minutes. Then, rub the loose skins off the chiles, over a sink, with running water. Rinse and dry. BE SURE NOT TO PUT YOUR FINGERS IN YOUR EYES WHILE HANDLING CHILES. (Or any other tender place!)

Another good warning is to cover any can of chiles containing juice with a towel while opening it. I once had a can squirt directly into my eyes with vinegar and chile oil. Painful!

The hotness of a chile comes from an oily substance called "capsaicin". It is generated in little globules on the inside ribs of the chile. If these are undisturbed, even the "hottest" chile will be like a sweet pepper in its meat and seeds. However, bumping, picking, packing or just the act of pulling it off the plant will rupture these fine globules allowing the burning hot oil to spread within the interior of the chile. Each chile . . . even on the same plant . . . has a little differing amount so don't count on uniformity of hotness from your chiles. Generally, the California Anaheim chiles have been bred to be least hot of the big green chiles marketed commercially. New Mexican friends do not remove all the seeds for they feel that seeds give a vitality and flavor which is important.

It's very easy to make a fine chile puree sauce with several pods of dried red chile. Often New Mexican families toast their dried red chiles in the oven a little while before making this puree. It does give a slightly different flavor. My preference is not to toast them. Try it both ways and decide for yourself.

BASIC RED CHILE PUREE

6-8 dried red chiles
½ cup water
½ teaspoon salt

½ teaspoon oregano
1 clove garlic, peeled

Take off the stem end and wash out the seeds. They are usually very hot. Then place the pods with the warm water into a blender. Add salt, oregano and garlic. Blend into a smooth puree and you will have the finest chile sauce. Try it over fried or scrambled eggs in the morning. (Hardly a home in New Mexico is without an electric blender.)

A good dish using this red chile is called CARNE ASADA.

CARNE ASADA
8-10 oz. medium-size cube of beef
¼ cup BASIC RED CHILE PUREE
   or ¼ cup pure ground chile powder
1 cup cooking oil

½ teaspoon garlic
½ teaspoon salt
½ teaspoon oregano

Take a cube of meat about four or five inches square. With a flat knife, cut it as one does meat when making JERKY . . . into a long strip about one-half inch thick and eight or nine inches long. Impale this on a wooden or metal skewer. Baste with BASIC PUREE or mix pure ground chile powder with hot water, then cooking oil and add garlic, salt, and oregano leaf. Swab the meat with the sauce while cooking. It barbecues the meat and has a deliciously bitey taste!

If you want a good lunch, fix a GREEN CHILE STEAK BOWL. The amounts are given per serving.

GREEN CHILE STEAK BOWL
3-4 oz. steak meat
1½ tablespoons butter
1 tablespoon flour
1 cup beef stock or water

½ clove garlic, fine-chopped or garlic salt
leaf oregano
½ cup green chile strips
salt, to taste

Take some steak meat, cut into bite-sized pieces, and saute it briefly in butter. Push meat to side and add flour to melted butter and mix well to make a roux. Add garlic and oregano. When hot and bubbly, pour beef stock or water over it, stir in, and make a moderately thick gravy. Add green chile strips cut into pieces. Cook fast for one minute and serve. This is good served with a salad and a flour tortilla.

A trinity of Indian foods

Southern Cheyenne maiden at Bent's Fort

Corn, beans, and squash comprise the trinity of Indian foods. Most important, corn provided the Indian with nourishment as food and drink. Husks were used as weaving material for food storage baskets.

The Plains Indians often dry the corn right on the cob. These are later soaked overnight before using, and taste almost as good as fresh corn. The southwestern Indians and New Mexicans sometimes steam cook their kernel corn and then dry it. These are called "chicos". . . or little ones. "Chicos" may be soaked overnight and then used as corn in any form of stew or vegetable dish.

Popcorn is not new. Over 5,000 years ago the Indians in Mexico used popped corn in strings for religious ceremonies. Even today, in remote Mexican churches one sometimes finds the statues of the Virgin or Christ decorated with strings of popcorn.

In George Herter's *Bull Cook and Authentic Historical Recipes and Practices* is a recipe for MOHAWK INDIAN CORN. This may or may not be Mohawk authentic, but Mr. Herter claims (and it's true) that the corn flavor is wonderfully amplified and improved by the addition of black walnut flavoring and black walnuts.

Raspberry and Blue Corn

MOHAWK INDIAN CORN

1 cup whole kernel corn, packed in water, frozen, or fresh, if available
1 small package black walnuts

½ teaspoon black-walnut flavoring
2 tablespoons butter
water

Empty corn into a heavy, cooking pot. Add black walnuts, sufficient water, and heat until corn is tender. When simmering, add the black walnut flavoring which is available at most grocery stores. Dot with butter and serve. It really is delicious.

When the settlers first came to America, they found Indians taking ashes from their fires, and pouring water through them to make a caustic solution. Dried kernel corn was then boiled in this ash water solution until the hard, outside shiny cover of the corn kernel floated loose. These were discarded and the uncovered kernel could be cooked or dried and ground into meal. In New England it was called "samp;" in the South, "hominy;" and among the Indians of Mexico, "nixtamal." Though hominy in its commercial canned state is rather dull and bland, when fixed in the Indian style with meat and herbs, it is magnificent. Ground hominy in the South is "grits," but in Mexico a similar corn meal is made into corn tortillas . . . the basic bread used in many forms of Mexican food (tostadas, enchiladas, tacos, etc.). This meal can also be toasted and used in various ways as you will see later in this book (PINOLE, chaquehue, CHAMPURRADO, WAS-NAH).

When cool weather comes to New Mexico, a favorite party dish or family get together meal is made of POSOLE (sometimes spelled pozole). It has such a wonderful heartiness and back-to-nature taste that you should experience it, however much you may be prejudiced against ordinary hominy. Here's how to make POSOLE.

POSOLE

2 cups dry posole or hominy
   or, 2 lbs. frozen or *wet* posole
   or, 4 cups of canned hominy (as a
   last resort, not very good)
4 lbs. pork shoulder cut into bite-
   sized cubes (use beef, if you prefer)

2 garlic cloves
1 teaspoon salt
1 teaspoon leaf oregano
½ teaspoon cumin
2 cups BASIC RED CHILE PUREE

Cook all ingredients together in a large, heavy pot. Let simmer for several hours until the corn "pops" open and serve with hot flour tortillas.

Many Indians and Southwesterners still use blue corn meal ground from the dark-colored Indian corn. Maiz azul (blue corn meal) is most often used for tortillas, but you will enjoy it in the old recipe for BLUE INDIAN CORN MEAL TAMALE PIE.

BLUE INDIAN CORN MEAL TAMALE PIE

2 cups blue corn meal
   or regular corn meal
water
2 lbs. ground beef or chunks of beef or game
   meat will make the dish even tastier
½ clove garlic, peeled, chopped fine
¼ teaspoon oregano, crushed
1 to 2 cups ripe olives, pitted, and chopped
2 cups water

1 can of tomatoes or a small can of
   tomato puree (optional)
3 cups grated longhorn cheese
   or 2 cups longhorn and
1 cup Montery Jack cheese, grated
1 or 2 tablespons red chile powder
   or 2 cups green chile strips
1 tablespoon flour

To make this pie, take a large pot and boil corn meal with enough water to make a mush. Cook the mush thick, being careful to stir it frequently, over a slow fire about 25 minutes. Do not use a glass pot as they have a tendency to burn, crack and break open if you're not watching carefully. (This happened to me while videotaping. Hot mush poured over the stove sending up clouds of smoke. Viewers thought it was terribly funny, but I was embarrassed.) While your mush is cooking, take a large frying pan and fry beef, onion, garlic, and oregano until beef is just barely cooked. Add some pure-ground red chile powder (1 to 2 table-spoons depending on how hot you like your food) or chopped green chile strips. Then add flour and stir. When all is well-mixed with the fat in the pan, and flour cooks a couple of minutes, add enough water to make a gravy. Though it's not authentic, I like to add a cup or two of pitted, ripe olives, sliced. If you like tomato flavor in your chile, add the tomatoes. Your meat sauce should look like a spaghetti sauce, but will be spicy from the chile. Now, look at the corn meal mush and if it is soft and well cooked, add 1 cup of grated longhorn cheese and stir into the mush. Next, using a dutch oven or baking casserole, pour in a layer of mush, sprinkle with more cheese, add a layer of meat, then more cheese, then mush . . . keep repeating until the casserole is full. Top with cheese and bake for an hour at 350%. (This dish can be served without being baked but baking greatly improves the flavor.)

Beans as used by the Indians came in many forms -the red; the black; the spotted pinto bean; the brown "bolito;" and of course the more familiar kidney, lima, and the Navy beans. In general, a bean needs to be soaked overnight before cooking.)

Pinto beans or FRIJOLES were and still are basic staples of western diet. When they're freshly-cooked, and NOT out of a can, pintos are some of the very best eating anywhere. It's just a shame that beans have a reputation for being a poor man's food, since they're so high in protein, nourishing and delicious. To cook them is simple enough.

FRIJOLES
2 cups dry pinto beans water to cover
3 strips bacon or ¼ lb. salt pork cut into ¼" cubes

Just boil the beans with bacon or salt pork in water for three hours or so, until soft. Cook at a slow simmer. If you must add water, be sure that it is warm water, or beans will harden. Serve with good RED CHILE PUREE, or red chile con carne, or just au natural.

The BOWL OF THE WIFE OF KIT CARSON is a superb "dry soup" from the Camino Real (the old Spanish Road to Mexico City from Santa Fe). Its proper

35

name is a caldo Tlalpeno, but Kit Carson's grand-daughter, Miss Leona Wood told me that she remembers eating it as a youngster. The "K.C. Bowl" (as we called it at The Fort) requires a special smoked chile pepper called the chile chipotle adobado, available from Mexican groceries in cans.

BOWL OF THE WIFE OF KIT CARSON   Per Serving

¼ cup cooked chicken or turkey meat in bite-sized pieces
¼ cooked rice
1 cup rich chicken broth
¼ cup cooked garbanzos

pinch leaf oregano
¼ chopped chipotle pepper
¼ avocado, sliced
¼ cup cubed Monterey Jack or Muenster cheese

Heat broth to boiling and add chicken, garbanzos, chipotle pepper, rice, and oregano. Serve in large individual bowls, and add cheese pieces and avocado just when serving.

Squash comes in many forms and every Indian home usually has a storage area where chunks of dried squash are kept. The most familiar squash that we know is the pumpkin. Here is a traditionally Indian recipe for BAKED STUFFED PUMPKIN.

BAKED STUFFED PUMPKIN

1 large pumpkin
3 tablespoons butter
salt
2 cups corn, fresh kernels or canned
2 cups green beans, sliced or cut into pieces

1 lb. hamburger meat
2 onions
2 fresh peaches, peeled (frozen or canned may be substituted)
1 cup cooked chicken meat
1 cup sunflower seeds or sunflower seed meal
1 cup green bell pepper, chopped

Take a large pumpkin, cut a fairly wide lid from the top (jack-o-lantern style). Use a scraping spoon to take out all the seeds and strings on the inside. Butter, salt and pepper the inside of the pumpkin; place in a 350° oven for about 40 minutes; do not put the lid on. Bake, but repeatedly check the inside of the pumpkin for an accumulation of juice will appear. Use a long ladle and empty it from time to time, or the pumpkin will collapse. Meanwhile, brown the hamburger with the onions in a large skillet. Add corn; beans; pepper; peaches cut into chunks; chicken meat; and hulled, toasted sunflower seeds or sunflower seed meal. (Lewis and Clark found the Sioux using sunflower seed meal in their dishes.) Cook this together for about an hour with just enough water to keep it moist. Salt and pepper to taste. Then serve the stew inside the baked pumpkin. It makes a dramatic dish when brought to the table. Spoon out the cooked walls of the pumpkin as you serve the stew. It makes a fun Halloween dinner dish.

Plains Indian desserts generally were made of berries. A broad term for a toasted corn dessert is "WAS-NAH". Sometimes you'll find Sioux who call a type of pemmican "Was-Nah". An older Sioux lady friend, whose name is *LOVES HORSES*, taught me this recipe for WAS-NAH.

WAS-NAH, INDIAN VERSION

2 cups toasted corn meal
½ lb. butter, or ground kidney
   fat for the authentic Indian version

2 cups brown sugar
1 cup fresh bing cherries,
   or fresh chokecherries

Puree cherries through food mill. If you use the Indian style, do not seed cherries first (but warn your guests). Toast corn meal on a cookie sheet in the oven. It toasts very rapidly, so don't let it burn. Stir it around so that it toasts evenly. Use the kidney fat from a buffalo or beef, and grind it fine. This fat is the best and purest found on an animal. Simmer in a pan to render oil. Mix this with the corn and brown sugar. Add chokecherries and mash everything together. This is the real recipe . . . but for a modern variation, take:

WAS-NAH, Modern Version

2 cups toasted corn meal

½ lb. soft butter

2 cups brown sugar

1 cup seeded bing cherries, fresh frozen or canned

Mix ingredients together and allow to chill in the refrigerator. Give each person a heaping tablespoonful. This is sweet and nourishing and makes a great snack for the kiddies. The toasted meal has something of the flavor of popped corn, and with the butter and sugar and cherries it is simply delicious.

Elizabeth Burt whose FORT LARAMIE CHICKEN SALAD has been given earlier, also had a recipe in her cookbook for BAKED INDIAN PUDDING. It is a very rich, heavy pudding. I prefer a lightly sweetened whipped cream to the sugared butter that Elizabeth recommends. The blender is modern but useful.

BAKED INDIAN PUDDING

1 quart milk

2 cups (1 pint) corn meal

1 cup (½ pint) molasses

1 tablespoon butter

⅛ cup sugar, beaten with butter

3 eggs

grated lemon peel

raisins

½ cup butter

Pour a quart of boiling milk over the corn meal. Let it cool. Heat the molasses and butter together. Whip eggs in blender, add lemon peel and pour in hot molasses while blender is running. Add the raisins and mix with the cornmeal. Bake slowly

38

at 325° for one and one-half hours in a covered pan within a larger pan of water in the oven to help keep the heavy cornmeal from burning. Eat with beaten butter and sugar. (Manuscript cookbook of Elizabeth Burt, Fort Laramie, Wyoming.)

Very few spices were used by the Plains Indians. Even salt was rare. Roasted coltsfoot herb was substituted for salt. Most of their foods featured just the flavor of corn, beans, squash, and meat.

I had read of a cooking technique used by the early Brule Sioux before they had metal kettles. This was once shown by their elders to young Sioux at a pow-wow in 1925. In Rosebud, South Dakota, in 1969, we were able to film the technique of using a beef paunch as an edible kettle. An old Brule Sioux named Carl Ironshell took the well-washed paunch from a newly killed beef and hung it from four posts driven into the ground. These were forked sticks at the top, and served to suspend the paunch or stomach at four corners . . . as a bag might be suspended with four legs at opposite corners. A hot wood fire was built nearby, and smooth stream-bed rocks placed in it to heat. Into the paunch were placed about 3 gallons of water, and several pounds of raw beef meat in bite-sized pieces. When the rocks were hot, they were lifted into the paunch, and by the time the fifth rock was dropped into the water, the liquid was boiling furiously. After repeating this procedure for an hour, the meat was cooked, the broth ready to be eaten. Following this repast, the paunch itself was eaten . . . mainly uncooked. It is not a dish to delight the fastidious gourmet, but interesting nonetheless as to ingenuity of the Indian cook's use of available materials as a cooking pot.

Brule Sioux Indians cooked food in a paunch using hot rocks before metal kettles were known.

Breads of the Frontier

Bread oven "horno" at Taos Pueblo in New Mexico

From the Atlantic coast westward, stomachs were nourished by a native American grass which we call corn. From prehistoric times, corn served as the basic ration of Indian peoples, and was adopted by the Frontiersmen as their basic food too. A handful of corn meal kept in a bladder was the "iron ration" of the Indian warrior.

Many types or variations of corn exist . . . from the small, three-inch-long, raspberry corn (the appearance of the kernel is similar to popcorn, except that it's scarlet in color) . . . to the long hybrid ears known today.

An interesting version of corn bread still found among the Indians of Arizona is called "piki." These are rolls of tissue-thin crisp corn, rolled up like a morning newspaper. Also in early days called "guayabes" by the Spanish, (perhaps because they looked like guavas to Mexican settlers) these pikis are made by cooking a thin corn-and-sage ash gruel on a hot rock. Almost instantly, when cooked, they're rolled up tightly. These may be colored with native yellow saffron or with red cockscomb. The most common color is a blue-black when piki is made from the blue Indian corn. When colored brightly and fastened together, the piki is known a Kachina food or food for the gods, and is delicious.

Blue corn meal (from slaked-lime-treated corn) is found most often among the Indians of New Mexico and Arizona. A few places produce it commercially, and it makes the very best corn tortillas. The flavor is exceptional.

Incidentally, that marvelous taste of modern corn chips, such as "Fritos", taco shells and other "Mexican corn products" comes not from a particular type of corn, but rather from the process of removing the hard covering with a slaked lime caustic procedure first. This is the secret of that great flavor found in Mexican food. There is a little bit of residual musty-scent lime after the corn has been washed many times which gives it that special flavor. When the corn is dried and ground into meal, it is called "nixtamal," and has the inimitable flavor of Mexican food. The meal, or "masa" may be mixed with water and a little salt, then made into thin cakes. These are cooked on a griddle and are called tortillas.

Tortillas also may be made with wheat flour; those are the tortillas used for burritos. Navajo and Hopi Indians also add a bit of wood ash to make balls of corn meal, and these are cooked in the coals, making a walnut-sized bread.

POTATO BREAD

6 medium Irish potatoes
2 cakes yeast, dissolved in 1 cup tepid water
1 teaspoon baking soda

4 cups flour, sifted
salt

Boil Irish potatoes until tender, peel and mash them. Then pour the water in which they were boiled over them and add a quart of cold water; stir in 2 cups of flour. Let it cool. Put in yeast and let it rise overnight. In the morning, strain the above through a colander and add enough flour to keep the sponge from adhering to the bowl. Stir in more flour to make it the consistency of a stiff batter, add soda, and let it rise again. After it is light, add salt and enough flour to knead it thoroughly, then let rise again and form into loaves. Let rise still another time, then put into the oven and bake 1 hour, at 350° to 375°. This makes 5 medium-sized loaves. (From the manuscript cookbook of Elizabeth Burt, Fort Laramie.)

Elizabeth Burt at Ft. Laramie, Wyoming.

Navajo woman in typical crushed velvet dress, adapted from mid-Victorian pioneer womens' dresses

Frontier desserts

Pies were a popular item in the Old West diet.

Man seems to have a sweet tooth, no matter where he comes from. The habit of having a sweet item for dessert was well known among the Europeans, and not unknown to the Indian. The New Mexicans, being a mixture culturally of the Spanish and the Indian, found that fruits with their natural sugars were the most readily available source of sweet. Although cane sugar and molasses were well known in the early West (coming from the Caribbean and from Mexico) they were luxuries which had to travel a long way on wagons. All the early fur-trade forts had molasses . . ."long sweet" as it was then called.

An old favorite dessert in New Mexico is CAPIROTADA. This is a bread pudding, often called "sopa." New Mexico was cut off from the rest of Mexico by the long distances involved. The missions in early days were supplied by a wagon train which came once every two years from Mexico. It brought wines, fruit, tree seeds and grape shoots, chocolate, cheeses and delicacies from Europe for the French or Spanish priests. It is quite likely that the many apple orchards of New Mexico grew from seeds brought from Europe in the very early days by priests. The dessert, CAPIROTADA, was encountered by the early mountain men and travelers to New Mexico from 1825 onward. They had trouble with Spanish, and preferred to call it "Spotted Dog" because of the raisins in the dish. A later variation of this dish was cooked by the chuckwagon cooks during the cattle period, and was called "Spotted Pup".

CAPIROTADA

2 cups toasted bread
4 eggs
2 cups milk
1 cup raisins in hot water
½ lb. brown sugar
2 tablespoons cinnamon

1 teaspon nutmeg
½ onion
½ lb. butter, melted
1 cup Longhorn cheese
2 cups sliced apples (optional)

Break up toasted bread, preferably old, dry bread. In another bowl, beat eggs well and add milk. Separately, put raisins in 1 cup hot water to cover. Allow to soak and plump for five minutes, and drain. Add dark-brown sugar to the milk-egg mixture and mix in with sliced apples. Add cinnamon, and nutmeg. Chop onion fine. Mix all thoroughly with the bread and moisten with butter melted in 2 cups hot water. Grate Longhorn cheese. Place layers of the pudding in a casserole, alternately with layers of the cheese. Bake at 350° about 45 minutes, and serve hot. Sprinkle with tiny, colorful cookie candies.

According to Stuart Berg Flexner, a noted scholar of the American language and American social history, the word "pie" meant a meat pie to the English and the first colonists to come to America. All used "tart" as their word for a pastry filled with fruit, berries, or jam. But the colonists were soon calling both dishes "pies" and eating both for breakfast. The word "pie" can be traced back to "pica", the Latin word for magpie, who fills its nest with miscellaneous objects, as do the English with their meat pies.

A familiar dessert pie of the Southerners who came west in early days was CHESS PIE. This was probably of English origin. Today it's usually found in southern states, and then only rarely. It's one of the simplest and best pies you can bake.

CHESS PIE

¾ cup sugar	1 lemon
2 tablespoons butter	4 eggs
pinch salt	

In a blender combine, butter, eggs, pinch salt, and thin outer rind plus cut-up pulp of lemon. Place in lightly baked pie shell and bake at 350% for 25-30 minutes.

Chess tarts and a chess cake, all pretty much the same recipe, are very old standards in early American cookbooks. Sometimes they'd put a big spoonful of some type of sharp jelly or preserve in the center of the tarts or pie.

Mrs. William Shannon of Broomfield, Colorado, provided us with her variation on our CHESS PIE. This is called TRANSPARENT PIE and came from the Virginia-Kentucky frontier period. It's easy and delicious.

TRANSPARENT PIE

1 pie crust	1 cup white sugar
8 ounces tart jelly	3 eggs
1 cup butter	

Bake a good pie crust in the oven until crisp. Then add the following filling: Cover the bottom of the pie crust with your favorite tart jelly. Cream butter with sugar. Add this to well-beaten eggs. Beat the mix until light and fluffy, then place over the jelly in the pie shell. Bake fast at 450° for five minutes; then reduce the heat to 375° for another 20-25 minutes. When the center of the filling is almost firm, remove from the oven and cool. The filling is somewhat transparent, and the jelly makes it just great eating.

At Fort Robinson, Nebraska, the famous old cavalry headquarters, I found a recipe for an APPLE PIE WITHOUT APPLES. It is a very good dish, and with the exception of the seeds, you cannot tell it from real apple pie. It shows the ingenuity of the early frontier cooks.

APPLE PIE WITHOUT APPLES

2 cups soda crackers

2 eggs

1 cup sugar or ½ cup honey

1 cup milk

3 teaspoons nutmeg

2 teaspoons cinnamon

½ lemon peel, grated

double-crust pie shell

Break up soda crackers and put them in the bottom of an unbaked 9" piecrust. In a blender, mix eggs, sugar or honey, milk, spices and grated lemon rind. Pour over the crackers and add top crust to pie. Bake about 40 minutes in a 325° oven. You won't be able to tell this from real apples! Good eating . . .

On the Sioux Indian reservation, the old people still make a dessert called WO-JAPI . . . pronounced Whoa-zha-pee. They take chokecherries when ripe in the fall and mash them together. Small cakes are formed of the berries and allowed to dry. Later, when these are to be used, the Indian soaks the cakes in water until soft and takes a stone mallet to mash the cake. It is placed into a kettle of water with flour and sugar and cooked into a dessert. The flour thickens the mixture. It is very good cold, although the seeds are crunchy and hard on the teeth. An easy and less chewy version is WHITE EYES' WO-JAPI.

WHITE-EYES' WO-JAPI

1 #7 can or package frozen boysenberries
   or blackberries
2 cups sugar
2 tablespoons flour

2 cups cold water
lemon peel, grated
whipped cream or ice cream

    Mix flour in cold water to a smooth, thin paste. Cook berries with water and sugar and add flour paste. Grate lemon peel into the mix. Allow to boil slowly until flour is cooked (about 15 minutes). Chill and serve. If you want to be sophisticated, add some whipped cream or ice cream on top. It's an easy and tasty dessert and can be kept for a long time in the refrigerator.

    One fine dessert or side dish eaten by the mountain men was called TRAPPER'S FRUIT. Use a package of dried apples which are available at every supermarket. Health food stores often have excellent honeycured dry apples and other fruits. The Pennsylvania Dutch markets also have "apfel schnitz" (dried apples) which are delicious in this dessert.

TRAPPERS FRUIT   (Serves 8)

2 lb. package of dried apples
2 cups of applesauce
3 tablespoons of honey
½ cup of nuts of your choice
2 tablespoons coriander seed

½ cup raisins
2 oz. dark rum
whipped cream
vanilla

    Boil the dry apples in applesauce, with honey, nuts, coriander seed and raisins. Cook over medium heat for approximately 15 minutes; then add dark rum. Serve hot in dessert bowls, topped with real whipped cream, flavored with a dash of vanilla.

Frontier drink

Life in the early forts of the West was not all so primitive as one might think. Although beaver tail, raw buffalo liver, and dog stew often graced the tables, the "Bourgeois" or boss-man of the fort was served food on English porcelain, and wiped his mouth with damask napkins. Most forts had wine cellars featuring French and Spanish wines. St. Julian Medoc Bordeaux wines from France, Tenerife wine from the Canary Islands, ports and sherries, clarets and fine Madeira vied with an occasional bottle of French champagne as favorites.

Wines were usually sold by the hogshead or "pipe" (2 hogsheads or 105 gallons). Wine was decanted from these barrels into blown-glass bottles, supplied empty to the buyer. Bottles were so rare on the frontier that the 25 cent bottle of whiskey sold in St. Louis could be drunk while on the Santa Fe Trail and the bottle sold empty for 50 cents in New Mexico!

Temperance organizations became very active in the 1820's. Large quantities of alcohol were shipped west for trade to Indians, Federal legislation was passed to prevent wholesale corruption of the Red Man. Eager for the dollar, a number of Americans set up stills in Taos, New Mexico, (then under Mexican rule) to make contraband liquor. This was called "Taos Lightning" and was a wheat whiskey. No one knows how much alcohol came north through trading, but with five distilleries in Taos running full-time by 1846, the amount must have been considerable.

Profits on alcohol were tremendous -sometimes amounting to a ten thousand percent profit. To mask the cutting of alcohol with large amounts of water, the early traders added gunpowder, red pepper, and tobacco tea.

INJUN WHISKEY

1 quart corn whiskey or Bourbon

3 or 4 hot red peppers

cut plug tobacco or tobacco from
  2 cigarettes

a thumb pinch of old-fashioned black gun powder, not modern nitrated gunpowder

1 cup water divided between two small
  cooking pots

Boil peppers for 10 minutes to make a tea in one pot of water. Do the same with the tobacco in a second pot. Strain and cook down by half. Add both to the whiskey and put a pinch of gunpowder into the bottle. The pinch of black gunpowder gives a special smooth taste. **Be sure to use the old-fashioned black powder made of saltpeter, sulphur, and charcoal, as modern nitrated high speed powders are poisonous.**

The Indians became used to this type of whiskey, and in the 1860's, when good whiskey finally came west, the Indians rejected it because it just didn't have the "good old flavor". Unscrupulous traders at Fort Laramie doctored their "Injun Whiskey" with laudanum (tincture of opium) in order to prevent violence among the Indians after heavy drinking. Some did over-dose and died.

During trading at Indian camps, the chief got to sample the contents of whiskey barrels to assure fellow tribesmen that it was worth the furs being traded. After the trades were concluded, the traders left camp before the whiskey was distributed, as they wished to avoid the violent party which inevitably followed.

A primitive mint julep was called the HAILSTORM and was traditionally served on the 4th of July at Bent's Fort, an 1830-period private fur trade fort located in southeastern Colorado. It was the hub of a vast Indian trade network and freighting business from Missouri to Santa Fe. Ice was taken from the nearby Arkansas River in the winter and stored in an ice house. Wild mint, known in

Spanish as "yerba buena" was found growing in the Spanish peaks to the west, and some type of whiskey was used. It may have been the Taos Lightning wheat-based whiskey or "Quentoque Juisque" (Kentucky whiskey as spelled by New Mexican customs officials).

HAILSTORM
per portion

½ liter or pint wide mouth canning jar with lid

3 ounces of Bourbon or Scotch whiskey

1 tablespoon powdered sugar

1 large sprig of fresh mint

cracked ice to fill jar

The HAILSTORM makes a marvelous party drink for you can put the mint, sugar and whiskey in the glass jars and seal them until the time of the party. Then all one needs do is to fill each with cracked ice and hand it to the guest. He shakes it lustily until the mint leaves are bruised, releasing their wonderful pungent flavors into the sweetened whiskey mix. Granulated sugar is nearly as good as powdered sugar for this purpose. Another advantage of the HAILSTORM is that for a party requiring controls on the amount of drinking, one each is a quite sufficient dosage.

Rum and applejack were extremely popular in early-day America. Together they make a fine drink called a "switchel". This is different from the HAYMAKER'S SWITCHEL which is a non-alchoholic summer drink made of molasses, vinegar and powdered ginger.

HAYMAKER'S SWITCHEL

¾ gallon of fresh cold water

½ cup light molasses

1 cup brown sugar

2 cups apple cider vinegar

Mix ingredients together and serve over ice. You may wish to add more molasses and taste it as you make it, for some vinegars are much stronger than others. It should be a pleasant sweet and sour spicy drink .

The temperance groups felt that applejack was a major public menace. They literally cut down hundreds of apple orchards throughout the country to prevent apple brandy from being made.

Champagne was not unknown in the West. Fort William, later known as Fort Laramie, was toasted with a bottle of champagne carefully brought west by a young man in 1832. In its later years as a major army post in eastern Wyoming, Fort Laramie boasted a wide range of fine liquors and foods including caviar!

You will find many references to drinking ATOLE as a basic Mexican Indian gruel. It is nothing more than thin corn mush. Nixtamal (masa harina) or ground hominy meal is cooked with water, or a meat stock. Chaquehue is thicker corn meal mush, no longer a beverage. Both ATOLE and Chaquehue are often enjoyed topped with a little red chile.

ATOLE

1 cup nixtamal (masa harina) or regular corn meal

3 cups meat stock or water

Cook ingredients over a low fire, stirring constantly until corn meal is soft.

There are many variations in terms in Mexican and Indian foods. Sometimes ATOLE is called PINOLE and vice versa but PINOLE is sweetened. A good historian will take terms in local cookbooks with some amount of suspicion for local terms are not necessarily universal ones. For example, in New Mexico, if you order "sopa" in a restaurant you will get a bread pudding dessert (similar to CAPRIOTADA). In Old Mexico, sopa means soup.

A delightful hot Mexican-Indian beverage is called PINOLE.

PINOLE

1 cup masa harina, or ordinary
   corn meal ground fine
¼ cup sugar

½ teaspoon powdered cinnamon
3 cups milk

Roast corn meal in a 450° oven for 4-6 minutes until golden brown, but not burned. Spread the meal evenly over a cookie sheet, and move it around twice while roasting by using a spoon. Cool, then add 1 part sugar to 4 parts corn meal, and flavor with powdered cinnamon. Add ½ cup cold water to moisten, then cook slowly in hot milk for about 15 minutes. Be careful not to let the meal burn on the bottom of your pot. Stir constantly. Use as much pinole mix to milk as you would hot chocolate mix to water in making a medium strong cup. This is healthful, nourishing and delicious to drink. When the corn meal is soft, pour into cups and drink. It's consistency should be the same as a medium thick cup of hot chocolate.

Champurrado is an extension of MEXICAN CHOCOLATE and PINOLE. Simply make PINOLE and add hot chocolate to it; combining the two drinks makes still the third, which is marvelously warming and nourishing.

Early visitors to the Southwest found the Mexicans enjoying a thick type of hot chocolate. It had both a different consistency and flavor than they had encountered elsewhere.

MEXICAN CHOCOLATE *is* different in that it has both cinnamon and a bit of vanilla in it, plus egg for festival occasions such as Christmas eve. You can make it very easily yourself.

MEXICAN CHOCOLATE

2 squares sweet chocolate
1 quart milk or cream
1 egg
½ teaspoon vanilla

pinch nutmeg
¼ teaspoon cinnamon
pinch ground, dry orange peel

Simply add hot milk or cream to sweet chocolate, add egg, vanilla, and cinnamon. Blend for 2 minutes. Start blender at slow speed, or the hot milk will jump at you! I like to add just a pinch of ground orange peel. Be sure, however you make it, to beat or blend until frothy. Top cups with nutmeg sprinkle.

The first commercial product of the English New World colonies was sassafras. The tree bark was used to make tea and the wood used in England for all sorts of containers . . . bible boxes, baby cradles and even in the construction of sailing ships because it was widely believed that ships built with sassafras wood were unsinkable. For a long period in England there was a commonly-held belief that sassafras also was miraculously good for people, that it cured stomach trouble, rheumatism and even made women fertile. Its popularity was so great and the demand for it so extensive that the Crown had a contract with the 1622 Jamestown Colony for 30 tons of sassafras. In fact, a man who did not produce his quota of 100 pounds of sassafras was fined in the amount of ten pounds of tobacco for his failure.

In the early American West, sassafras tea was a regularly used tonic, and was sought after by mountain man and pioneer alike. Today one still finds sassafras tea in herb counters of fancy groceries and in health food stores. It makes a delicious tea and you will find many older persons who swear by it.

Although coffee was known in the Middle East at the time of Christ, the great vogue for coffee houses in Europe did not come until the 18th Century. It soon spread to America. The first taverns, as we know them, originally were coffee houses which also sold liquor.

During the mid-1800's, both coffee and tea were thought to have medicinal value and were advised for prevention of headaches, gout, and "gravel." In point of fact, tea, that popular British, sea-going drink, probably did contribute, at least indirectly, to the health of sailors. They were admonished to use lemon or lime with it, and thus prevented scurvy.

Coffee beans were sold green to users until shortly after the Civil War. Roasting and grinding was up to the buyer. However, at that time, the Arbuckle Brothers in Pittsburgh, Pennsylvania, evolved a method of coating roasted coffee beans with a mixture of egg white and sugar. This prevented oxydation, held in roasted flavor, and the beans could then be shipped roasted to the consumer.

Arbuckles became quite famous in the West. In fact, the name was synonymous with coffee, and cowboys were known to speculate gloomily that coffee might not be available after the Arbuckles themselves died. At one time, each brown paper bag of Arbuckles coffee had a stick of peppermint candy included as a premium. Cowboys would be more than happy to grind the coffee beans in order to get the candy. Sometimes they even indulged in fisticuffs for it.

In addition to the peppermint, Arbuckles offered a second premium. The labels from the packages could be redeemed for men's razors, alarm clocks, and the like.

CAMPFIRE COFFEE . . . Old Style

1 quart cold water
1 cup ground coffee

1 egg
½ cup cold water

Heat a pot of cold water to boiling. (Allow to boil only 2-3 minutes.) Take a cup of ground coffee and an egg, then place them in the middle of a piece of cheesecloth. Tie into a sack, then break the egg in the sack by rapping it. Massage the bag to mix the egg with the coffee, then drop all into the boiling water. Cook for 4 minutes. Add ½ cup cold water to settle any grounds. The coffee is absolutely superb.

Typical Spanish "Californio" house, now a museum in San Diego.

Fur trapper with a pint jug of Taos Lightning

Mormon foods

Mormon hand-cart pioneers at "nooning" meal. The hat of the woman resembles the 20th century "Flapper" mode, but is historically correct.

From its founding in 1830, Mormonism has been a missionary religion, and "gathering to Zion" became a powerful force that brought thousands of enthusiastic converts to "The Promised Land" in Utah. The zeal of these Saints grew to such a high pitch at the middle of the nineteenth century that they offered "to walk from their homes in Liverpool, and from New York to the Great Salt Lake."

Thousands of poor persons in England, Ireland, Scotland, Denmark, Sweden, and Switzerland heeded the call to America and "The Promised Land." However, by 1855, following drouths and grasshopper plagues, both money and food were scarce, and only one-in-twenty who wanted to come to Utah could be brought there. A new plan was evolved by Brigham Young to bring the emigrants from the east coast by rail to Iowa City, Iowa, and thence to Utah pushing their possessions in handcarts across the plains and mountains.

The first of the heroic handcart companies came west in the summer of 1856. Tragedy struck the Saints who were in the last two groups to cross the plains that year. They were too late in the season. Snow and cold decimated them. Starvation was severe.

One traveler wrote, "Hitherto, although a ration of a pound of flour had been served out daily to each person, it was found insufficient to satisfy the cravings of hunger. Shortly after leaving Fort Laramie it became necessary to shorten our rations that they might hold out and that the company not be reduced to starvation. First the pound of flour was reduced to three-fourths, then to a half pound, and afterward to still less per day. However we pushed ahead."

One group was reduced to eating rawhide. At first it made them sick. Jones, a professional cook, devised a plan to make rawhide palatable. "Scorch and scrape the hair off; this has a tendency to kill and purify the bad taste that scalding gave it. After scraping, boil one hour, throwing the water away that had extracted all the glue, then wash and let it get cold, and then eat with a little sugar sprinkled on it."

Ten companies of the Saints traveled the handcart route between 1856 and 1860. The dedication and heroism of these travelers has rarely been equalled in the history of man. In later years the culinary heritage of the New Englanders, those from the British Isles, Scandinavia, and Switzerland formed the nucleus of now-famous Mormon cooking. Old recipes were adapted to the foods found in the countryside. One such is FRUIT SOUP which originated in Scandinavia.

FRUIT SOUP

1 pound of raisins	6 apples
pound of prunes	juice of ½ lemon
½ pound currants	sugar
½ pound red raspberries	1 tablespoon small white sago (or cornstarch)

Simmer the raisins, prunes, currants, raspberries, apples and lemon juice together with water for three hours. Add sugar to taste and cinnamon sticks. Then add sago to thicken and cook a few minutes more. Serve either hot or cold. It will keep a long time in the refrigerator. This may be served at the beginning of a meal or as a dessert.

Sago is a kind of starch produced from the stem of a West Indian palm. It is a wholesome, nutritious food and has long had a place in American cooking. George Washington, for example, had a sago palm.

Rhubarb was one of the Mormon mainstays. Settlers traveling west brought rhubarb roots wrapped in dampened cloths, or packed in a can of dirt. The vitamin-filled root provided protection against scurvy. RHUBARB PUDDING made with sago was an authentic and delicious Mormon dish.

SAGO-RHUBARB PUDDING

1 cup small white sago (called Pearl)
1 quart tepid water
pinch of salt

1 pound cooked fresh or frozen rhubarb
sugar to taste

Place small, white sago in a quart of tepid water with a pinch of salt, and soak for one hour. Boil and stir the sago until clear, adding water to make it thin. Then pour over cooked fresh or frozen rhubarb. Add sugar to taste, and cook for 2 or 3 more minutes. Remove from heat. Serve warm or chilled. Four portions.

Saints from New England brought an old Vermont recipe with them. It reputedly was popular with Ethan Allen and his Green Mountain Boys of the American Revolution. It is called RED FLANNEL HASH.

RED FLANNEL HASH

3 medium cooked beets, peeled
large cooked potato, peeled
1 pound ground chuck steak
salt and pepper to taste

6 tablespoons butter
1 medium onion, chopped
2 tablespoons cream

Chop beets with one large cooked potato into small cubes. Mix well with ground chuck steak. Add salt and pepper to taste. Melt 4 tablespoons butter in a large skillet, add chopped onion and cook until onions are clear. Stir in the meat/vegetable mix and fry until the meat is moderately cooked. Then put it all into a flat baking dish. Melt 2 tablespoons butter in cream and pour this over the hash. Put the baking dish under a broiler for a few minutes until the hash has a good crispy crust. If you don't have an overhead broiler, simply fry the hash in the skillet until a crust forms on the bottom. Turn it with a spatula from time to time. This is a good breakfast or supper dish, especially with fried or poached eggs on top.

FINKER

2 lb. pork kidney fat
4 diced apples
2 medium onions

1 lb. beef or buffalo liver
1 lb. beef heart

Render kidney fat to cracklings, then grind with cooked liver and boiled heart. Brown in a wide fryingpan with diced apples, two chopped onions, salt and pepper. Serve warm with fresh vegetables.

COLCANNON

4 medium potatoes, boiled and mashed
1 cup cooked, chopped spinach

2 tablespoons butter
salt and pepper

Mix mashed potatoes with drained, cooked, spinach, butter, salt and pepper. Put into a greased mould, then bake ten minutes at 375°.

POTATO BALLS

4 medium potatoes, mashed
1 egg yolk

1 egg, beaten
½ cup cracker crumbs

Mix an egg yolk with mashed potatoes, then form balls (golf ball size). Dip in beaten egg and cracker crumbs, then fry in oil or brown in a Dutch oven.

(The above two of my favorite Mormon recipes from *The Pioneer Cookbook*, 1961 Kate B. Carter, Utah Printing Co., Salt Lake City, Utah)

A story is told of the earliest Mormon women faced with the problem of finding a sugar substitute. From a hole cut in the top, they cleaned the insides of ripe pumpkins of seeds and pulp. Then the pumpkins were left outdoors during cold nights for several days. The juices of the pumpkins gathered within them, and were removed for boiling into a sugary syrup.

Trappers in the West carried very little food with them. Rice, corn meal, flour, raisins, dried fruit, sugar, salt pork, and coffee were staples. Sugar was a great delicacy, and often honey was used in its place. It should be noted, however, that honey was not native to the land. The honey bee was brought from England to the New World. In fact, the Indian usually knew it was time to move west ahead of the white man when he saw the honey bee ranging into his territory. Records exist of the Spanish in California and later of the Mormons in Utah finding "manna" or a sweet crystaline substance on the leaves of certain trees. This came to be known as "Mormon sugar," and was only recently identified as the droppings of aphid insects.

Christmas specials

Christmas-time in old Santa Fe is a delightful experience. The cool crisp winter air is perfumed with smoke from pinon (Spanish pine) or native cedar fires. On Christmas Eve, many Santa Feans travel south about forty miles to a wonderful Indian pueblo called San Felipe. My most vivid memory of a Christmas Eve was in 1948 when I arrived at the pueblo at about eleven that night. The little church was lit with oil lamps and candles. For about twenty minutes the Indians in costume danced up to the altar in a serious prayer ceremony. Then the priest arrived for the midnight Mass. It was a moving experience. Later we went to Joe Esquibel's house for BISCOCHITOS. These wonderful, anise-cinnamon flavored cookies made a perfect combination with steaming hot coffee brewed from clear Indian pueblo's well water. Here's a good recipe for BISCOCHITOS.

BISCOCHITOS

6 eggs

1 pound lard, or solid shortening

4 cups sifted flour

2 cups sugar

2 tablespoons anise seed

rum or Bourbon

cinnamon

Beat eggs. In another bowl mix lard with flour. Cream sugar into the flour-lard mix. Mix in the eggs and anise seeds, and add sufficient flour to make a firm dough. Roll out and cut into your favorite cookie shapes. Rub tops of cookies with rum or Bourbon, then sprinkle with cinnamon. Bake at 375° for about three to five minutes, or until barely brown. Serve with hot coffee.

Another Christmas tradition in New Mexico is the use of ``farolitos'' and ``luminarias''. Farolitos or little lanterns are easily made by using brown paper bags. Fold down the top of the sack about 2 inches. This firms the sack. Then place about 3 cups of sand (or kitty litter) inside, and put a long-burning candle in the sand. When placed along walks, on porches, or along roof lines, these farolitos shine a cheery, yellowish light at night which delights the eye.

Many people mistakenly call farolitos by the name "luminarias." Luminarias are crossed square stacks of pitch pine wood, lit for a bright bonfire. These were used in Spain by the Moors long before the Christian religion arrived there. They are an old Spanish tradition.

The Spanish pine (pinon) produces a fine small nut. These can be obtained commercially, or gathered and roasted by yourself. (Some New Mexicans wait for the first snow, then follow ground squirrel or chipmunk trails to underground burrows where pinons are stashed in quantity for the coming winter. Nice people leave some for the animals!) Pinon nuts are best hulled after roasting by cracking the shells in your teeth. It takes a lot of Indian children to do it, but a good New Mexican HOLIDAY BIRD STUFFING may be made by combining the following:

HOLIDAY BIRD STUFFING

4 chopped fresh apples	1 cup mashed potatoes
1 dozen eggs	1 cup roasted, shelled pinon nuts
1 chopped onion	4 cups dry bread or bread pieces
1 tablespoon thyme	2 tablespoons sage
milk or water	1 cup diced green chiles

Add enough milk or water to the rest of the ingredients to make a moist mixture. Stuff this into a buttered fowl, or bake in a buttered pan. The eatin's great!

CHERRY BOUNCE is one of my favorite western Christmas memories. It is related to the early American "shrubs" which were combinations of fruit and brandy or rum. CHERRY BOUNCE is almost a liqueur when made properly.

CHERRY BOUNCE

5 pints dark cherries   1 pound brown sugar
1 quart dark rum or cognac

Grind cherries through a meat grinder, seeds and all. Place them in a bottle of dark rum or cognac. Allow to rest for one week. Then strain through a cheese cloth, and add brown sugar. Place in a jug and cork. Wait for two weeks before sipping yourself into Paradise. CHERRY BOUNCE is an early American recipe that'll really make history come to life for your holiday guests!

Punch as a drink came from the East Indian word *panch* meaning "five". During the 1600's, seamen drank panch made from five ingredients: tea, water, arrack, sugar, and lemon. Arrack (an Oriental liquor made from palm sugar) was replaced with rum in the 1700's, and rum punch survives today as a major holiday item.

Old Christmas drinks were generally much higher in protein than in alcohol. The two American favorites were: HANGMAN'S EGG NOG and YARD OF FLANNEL.

The HANGMAN'S EGG NOG came from the name "noggin." That was the term used for a solid wooden cylinder of birch made into a drinking container. Noggins were used at table while tankards, made from staves and hoops, were served at fireside. The present-day egg nog began its history as a "Dry Sack posset." "Dry Sack" was the English name for Spanish dry wine, primarily sherry. A dry wine was heated and mixed with eggs. Here is the old time HANGMAN'S EGG NOG that didn't come from a paper carton.

HANGMAN'S EGG NOG

6 eggs, separated
½ cup sugar
½ cup Jamaica rum
1 cup Bourbon

1 pint milk
½ pint whipped cream
nutmeg

Separate eggs and beat whites stiff and yolks until lemon colored. Add sugar to the yolks and stir. Place egg yolk and sugar mix in a large punch bowl; add rum, Bourbon, milk, and whipped cream. Then fold in the stiff egg whites and top with nutmeg. It is rich and delicious and was traditionally drunk after a hanging.

A fine favorite in taverns was called a YARD OF FLANNEL. It was so named because of the silky texture of this hot ale drink.

YARD OF FLANNEL

1 quart of good ale
4 eggs
4 tablespoons sugar

1 teaspoon ginger or grated nutmeg
½ cup Jamaica dark rum

Heat ale in a saucepan. Beat eggs with sugar. Add ginger or grated nutmeg, then rum. When the ale is almost boiling, combine the two mixtures, pouring the hot ale a little at a time into the egg mixture to prevent curdling. Pour these back and forth until it is silky and like "flannel." This is a wonderful holiday drink that was a great favorite with the coachmen, outriders, and wagoneers. It sounds far more complicated than it is, and the small effort is worth it in inner warming.

Index